T0356743

How to Date Your Wardrobe

How to Date Your Wardrobe

AND OTHER WAYS TO REVIVE, REVITALIZE, AND REINVIGORATE YOUR STYLE

Heather Newberger

HarperCollins books may be purchased for educational, business, or sales promotional use. For information, please email the Special Markets Department at SPsales@harpercollins.com.

FIRST EDITION

Designed by Elina Cohen
Illustrated by Hilary Fitzgerald Campbell

Library of Congress Cataloging-in-Publication Data has been applied for.

ISBN 978-0-06-302734-3

21 22 23 24 25 LSC 10 9 8 7 6 5 4 3 2 1

For you.

Yes, You.

CONTENTS

How to Date Your Wardrobe

INTRODUCTION

Have you ever tried reimagining your wardrobe, only to encounter unexpected roadblocks along the way? From figuring out your frame to developing a point of view, when it comes to your personal style, taking a closer look at the way you approach things can easily turn into a chore. But you're not alone. Uncovering how you feel about fashion can be an intimidating process for more reasons than you may realize.

With minimal effort, it can transform the way you see yourself. However, unfortunately, when I explain to people how easy it is to change their opinions of themselves just by adjusting what they put on in the morning, they often roll their eyes and tell me they don't care about fashion, as if by saying that, they can negate the impact it has on their lives.

I intimately understand this. It's much easier to disengage from something that makes you feel unwanted than admit it hurts you that way. But you don't have to live in fear of the dressing room's critical eye.

When we struggle to combat a persistent issue, it's often because we are continually coming at it from the same angle, without taking time to reconsider our approach. Instead of finding yourself frustrated every time you struggle to put together a new outfit, I urge you to take another look at the way you think about the body wearing it.

Only when you're ready to make a conscious effort to accept your figure, are you truly prepared to dress it. My hope is that you will use this book to revive your relationship with your wardrobe, so you have space to revitalize your perspective, to ultimately reinvigorate your attitude not only about your style—but yourself.

• • •

I was a healthy six feet when I entered high school, and desperate to fit in while my body begged to stand out. Among the five-foot-seven athletes and "popular" kids, I was quick to find fault with my tall frame. It required me to think differently about the way I dressed, and demanded I push up the sleeves of all my long shirts so no one could tell the cuffs barely skimmed my wrists.

I spent hours obsessing over the styles of the girls I'd see walking down the hallway, lusting after the outfits they wore. But instead of reexamining my own insecurities, I undermined myself by blaming my stature and womanly hips for not being asked to parties.

I still remember a trip I took to Hollister where I tried to purchase a skirt I'd seen one of my classmates wearing. I'd saved for weeks to afford it, and anticipated the day it would be mine. It was a green wraparound with white polka dots that I was certain, once in my possession, would change my life for the better. But when I tried it on in the dressing room, even the largest size wouldn't fit. It was too short for my tall frame. The white triangle of my underwear sticking out from the bottom, my fleshy hips spilling out of the sides. I immediately knew I would never look like my classmate. But even worse—when I stood in front of the dressing room mirror, I hardly recognized the person staring back.

All these years later I still remember the sinking feeling I had leaving the heavily perfumed store. I felt like I would never measure up to my classmates, and not being able to purchase that skirt reaffirmed what I was so afraid of being true: that my body would always keep me from becoming the person I was meant to be.

I wish my story was unique, but if I've learned anything over the past fifteen years, it's that this story isn't just mine—it's also my mother's and my friends', and I bet it's yours, too. It's the story of every person who has ever been told that to thrive, you must fit within an existing framework that has been created without your needs in mind.

Not seeing yourself in a flattering light can quickly eat away at self-confidence. And it's these types of encounters that paralyze us from trying new cuts, new stores, and new designers. Over time, our bad experiences coalesce into negative opinions about fashion, which can make you feel as though the least painful way to move forward is to reject the notion it's important to you at all.

For years, I flew blindly through the landscape, yearning to see bodies like mine in the media, aching to receive a road map that would teach me how to dress. I was exhausted from all the times I'd had to creatively find ways to hide my insecurities. However, as the years went on, I realized no one else was going to do my heavy lifting. And it is that very creativity which has made me a successful stylist today. In having to figure out how to feel confident in my own skin, I created tricks that could be passed along and I now use professionally. No longer do I consider myself a victim of circumstance. As a stylist, I put my experiences to good use.

In many ways, this book is an amalgamation of all the responses I've ever given, or wish I could have given, during conversations on set; with personal clients, my friends, family; or even while chatting with a random guy at a party. When someone finds out you're a stylist, they can't wait to pick your brain. But after our talk, I am rarely if ever afforded an opportunity to walk with them toward their goal. Confidence in your style expands and contracts with your ability to accept yourself, and it's that muscle I want to work with you to grow.

Every time we put on clothes, we communicate our intentions, decisions, desires, and needs. We tell our personal narratives through the cuts of our jackets and our histories with our shoes. So why, instead of embracing the inevitable, do so many of us allow our individuality to be suppressed by fear?

The goal of this book is to equip you with the tools you need to repair your relationship with your wardrobe. It's not about what will look good on your pear- or apple-shaped figure. It's designed to inspire you to throw out the fruit basket altogether. Because it's only when we are ready to accept our bodies that we can begin to dress them.

What you want
should not be determined by
what you're getting.

revive

Every time we think of a memory we corrupt it. When we recall our pasts, scientists suggest we recontextualize them and often shift our narratives toward ones that inform the people we have become, as opposed to who we were at the time.

Unfortunately, our closets rarely follow our personal growth, and frequently leave us wearing things that may have once helped to tell our stories but no longer fit our needs. We all have a couple of tops or pairs of jeans we won't get rid of because we feel we spent too much money on them, or we loved them so much at one time. But you're never going to wear that cowboy-inspired red-ruffled button-down again, are you?

Each of us has a relationship with our wardrobe, whether we're comfortable saying we "care about fashion" or not. Through thick and thin, our closets are always by our sides—even when we feel the choices they present are less than ideal.

Which is why it's so important to put energy into reviving your relationship before you think about how you would like to reinvent it. Instead of throwing your hands in the air and getting frustrated before you even start, I want you to figure out what excites you, what doesn't, and all the nooks and crannies in between.

In this section we'll go over how to get rid of those difficult garments while reintroducing you to your style, so you can embrace the person you've become and close the chapter on who you were before.

EMBRACE YOUR INSECURITIES

All day, every day, we keep running narratives in our heads that get constantly added to and rearranged, depending on our experiences. These autobiographies help us understand what's around us, but they also distort the lens through which we see each other and, most importantly, ourselves. This is the place where self-doubt can often fester and balloon without our knowledge.

Before you can fully revive your relationship with your wardrobe, you have to take a hard look at all the nasty insecurities that have wormed their way into your story. These doubts

are often critical in shaping the way we see ourselves and hold us back from accepting the people we are today.

It's easy to lust after the past. Even if not all of your experiences felt great at the time, remembering them does offer an ineffable sanctuary the future does not present. The unknown is scary. But it's also filled with so much possibility for you to take advantage of.

When it comes to our personal styles, we must embrace what makes us anxious so that we can highlight the things that don't. Do your wide hips make you nervous? They're also the reason your waist looks so small.

When you take time to accept your insecurities, you make space to think about how you can creatively tackle them. Give yourself the room to say—this is what I want to call attention to, and this is what I don't. By assuming responsibility for your body, you regain control of your appearance in a way that allows you to be confident in whatever decisions you make.

Everyone has something they don't love about themselves—whether it be frustrations with our arms or the length of our legs. I once had a client who hated her neck, so everything we dressed her in had to hide it. I thought her neck was beautiful, but your insecurities aren't about how other people see you—they're all about how you see yourself.

We each have different bodies, come from different experiences, and have different expectations for how we would like our garments to fit. Which is why it would be silly for me to suggest you can easily let go of your existing mindset, wipe away every piece of negative self-talk, and move forward without taking a moment to comb through your experiences. So instead of attempting to ignore your anxieties, try taking a step back and evaluating them at face value.

Ask yourself, What does my point of view say about how I look at the world? And why do these things affect the way I see myself in the mirror? The way we think about ourselves is often the exact opposite of how our friends and families do.

So try pretending you're somebody who loves you. What would they say?

EXPAND YOUR EXPECTATIONS

A few years ago during a re-watch of *Veronica Mars*, I realized that in one of the episodes, she wears a jacket just like one I used to own. I thought it was funny and texted my friends, but quickly realized there was more to the story. At the time of the show's original airing, I was a teenager much like Mars, and was attracted to her strong will, confidence, and ease giving a little sass. Without being cognizant of it, I'd chosen to emulate her style in hopes I could adapt the same attitude. But in doing so I forgot to consider if my outfits looked good on *me*.

Though it took years to divorce myself from Veronica's choices, once I was able to, I found myself struggling to figure out what I wanted to say. With the pressure suddenly on my shoulders, I found it easier to tell people fashion just wasn't for me, instead of examining what my preferences actually looked like.

Many of us feel like there are only a few types of clothing we're allowed to wear, given our figures or age—but we're not necessarily responsible for those points of view. More often than not, our attitudes toward what we wear and how our clothing makes us look have been shaped by the media and the picture-perfect models we see on billboards. Lusting after someone else's style can be helpful for inspiration, but when it comes to dressing your own body, it can frequently lead to cluttered closets filled with garments that may look better on someone else.

So stop undermining yourself by thinking only some things are acceptable for the person you are. The way you dress is a performative act, but it's a performance worth watching only if it's honest and unflinchingly yours. Because no matter how much you might feel like someone has put you in a box, the perimeters of your wardrobe have been designed by one person, and one person only—and that's you.

Everything you choose to wear signifies something about who you are, from the color of your glasses down to the style of your shoes. Which is why it's so important to select only articles of clothing that help you author a story you're excited about.

Because I was so concerned about hiding the aspects of my body I saw as flaws, I held myself back from thinking there may be some things I'd like to highlight, too. However, once I was able to take a moment to remove myself, and make time to identify my concerns, the things I love about my body began to seamlessly reveal themselves.

Critically considering what you want to communicate may feel overwhelming at the start, but it's the only way you can take full ownership of your closet and your choices. When you focus on someone else's decisions, you're wasting time you could be devoting to developing your own point of view.

As soon as I was able to see my body as separate from others', I was able to tackle my insecurities without fear. Ownership breeds confidence, and the more self-assured I became, the easier it was for me to try new things and reject them—without the process feeling personal.

Once you find one thing you like about yourself, it becomes a lot easier to find more. Let go of the idea that whatever you choose has to fit within a specific framework, especially if it looks (and feels!) right on you.

pro tip! ADMONISH YOUR ANXIETIES

I've always found putting my thoughts on paper to be helpful when defining my needs—especially when I notice myself struggling to articulate them. There is a big difference between thinking something and seeing it in front of you that can cement your point of view.

Instead of trying to remember everything that's ever bothered you about your body, try listing five things that make you anxious in this very moment. Then, write down five ways you can subvert the way you think about them. You may have to do this a few different times, but just by seeing what words you decide to put on paper, you'll begin to discover where your bias lies.

1. ______________________________

Turn it on its head: ______________

2. ______________________________

Try something different: ______________

3. ______________________________

Take a new approach: ______________

4. ______________________________

Tell yourself a different story: ______________

5. ______________________________

Test out a fresh point of view: ______________

Pro Tip: Size Is Just a Number

The sizes retailers place on garments are often arbitrary and unique to their brand, which makes size one of the most frustrating hurdles to overcome when getting in touch with your personal style. Unsurprisingly, these numbers often lead to disappointment and anger when something that "says" it should look good on you just . . . doesn't.

The way a garment fits is more important than whatever size is listed on its tag, but without a realistic framework in place, how can you possibly figure out which pieces will look right on your body without wasting hours of your day?

Every person is built differently, which means there are no Traveling Pants, or garments that flatter every frame. Instead, it's up to you to try, try, and try again, until you get a sense of what feels authentic on your body and you're able to buck the notion that the size tag sewn inside a garment holds any value at all.

It's a small step, but even cutting out that tag can offer a bit of relief if you'd rather never see it again. Focus instead on how the garment falls on your figure and if it communicates what you want it to.

Our insecurities aren't easy to shed, but one way we can start the process is by stopping ourselves from undermining our personal preferences. Quit holding yourself back from trying on that shirt because you're not a fan of what size the tag says. The only thing that really matters is how it makes you feel.

HOW TO DATE YOUR WARDROBE

Your wardrobe has developed over time to meet the needs of all the different people you have been during your lifetime. But if you've picked up this book, you likely suspect your closet no longer aligns with the individual you are today. To own a wardrobe is to be responsible for maintaining something that is ever evolving, and you need to become comfortable adding to and subtracting from it as frequently as is required.

Instead of continuing to wear the same tired old pants, I urge you to ask yourself why you fell in love with them to begin with. Is it because they flatter your body a certain way? Because someone once told you they made your butt look great? Or because one day you didn't have anything else to wear, so you put them on and never looked back?

It's easy to allow your desire for *something* to distract you from finding the *right thing*, so try to get in touch with the person who bought those pants and the one who made the decision to keep wearing them.

Just remember—you might have feelings about your clothes, but your clothes don't have feelings. It can be informative to figure out your motivations behind previous choices you're not proud of, so in the future you can be more uncompromising and make better ones.

In romantic relationships, I struggled for years to learn the power of saying no. Instead of being selective with my partners and holding out for someone who was the right fit, I settled for the men who were interested in me, as opposed to the ones I was interested in dating—just because it felt flattering to be wanted.

Only after I took the time to identify what I desired from a relationship was I able to reclaim my dating life and connect with someone whose interests aligned with mine. But it didn't happen immediately. I still had to go on a lot of dates and tell a lot of people I wasn't interested in them, no matter how attractive I thought they were or how much money they made. I had to let go of these potential partners because they had qualities that didn't meet my needs, and everyone deserves to be with someone who does.

What you want should not be determined by what you're getting, and you have to have the same (uncomfortable) conversations with your wardrobe I had with these men. Not every person or piece of clothing is going to be a match, but it's up to you to say no until you find something (or someone) worth saying yes to.

Pro Tip: Reject Rejection

Sometimes you meet a garment that excites you the same way a potential partner can. When this happens, your mind unconsciously ascribes meaning to it—and when the garment does not fit the way you would like it to, the despair you experience can frequently feel as painful as a breakup. You imagine how much better your life would look with this item in it, but unfortunately, this is often a case where your brain gets ahead of your body and is responsible for creating futures you have no evidence to back up.

The more you run into this roadblock, the harder it can be to motivate yourself to get back out there without feeling dismal—especially when you feel you're finally starting to find your footing.

Instead of blaming yourself, try examining why the garment doesn't fit your needs. Was it poorly constructed? Created for a different body type? Or just one of those pieces that looks great on the rack but leaves a lot to the imagination once it's on you?

Regardless, you didn't do anything wrong—no matter how easy it is to look inward and blame yourself. Instead of getting frustrated, use this experience as a learning opportunity. Don't try to make the garment work or think sheer will can. Reject it and move on. The future you've imagined is still out there. You'll just be wearing something different.

CLEAR OUT YOUR CLOSET

Everyone uses objects to preserve memories. However, when we hold on to things that no longer serve us, we prevent ourselves from taking inventory of our current selves and can easily become paralyzed when we have to create space for the people we have evolved to be.

Instead of allowing yourself to be overwhelmed, thinking you need to overhaul your wardrobe (or your life!), here is a quick and dirty method I use whenever I need to take back ownership of my own closet:

First—I identify my favorite outfit—you already know what yours is. It's the one that makes you feel like a million dollars, and you've worn twice this month. Next, I'll set aside time to go through my closet and try on everything I have. Then I'll assess whether what I'm wearing makes me feel as good or not as good as my favorite ensemble does.

Every time you get that fuzzy feeling, I suggest you put the garment in Pile A, and if you find yourself thinking for a second too long, it goes in Pile B. Finally—it's important to move fast, before you can second-guess yourself—take Pile B to a local secondhand store or sell it immediately through an online retailer like Poshmark, thredUP, Depop, or Etsy.

You never know if your too short pants could be the perfect fit for someone's next job interview, or if a top that never felt right on you is exactly what another individual has been looking for. And if you're ever struggling to make a choice, remind yourself that by creating space for your needs, you're also allowing someone else to fulfill theirs.

It's easy to let
your desire for something
distract you from finding
the right thing.

revitalize

Once you've taken a minute to get in touch with your current self, it's time to hit the (metaphorical) pavement. Hopefully the previous section has given you a little more insight into what you like, why you like it, and how important it is to make your past work for your present.

Now that you're more aware of what your needs are, we can start looking at how to meet them with renewed energy and enthusiasm.

Your wardrobe has been patiently waiting for you to rev up its bones and give it a new lease on life, to revitalize it with a sense of authenticity that reflects the person you are today.

After all, isn't it about time you took control of the things you want, instead of allowing them to control you?

In this section I'll teach you how to zero in on your personal style, put intention behind your choices, and give you a behind-the-scenes look at how to shop smarter, not harder.

MODIFY YOUR MOOD

Amid our cluttered climate of online personalities and individualized branding, our clothing choices have become critical in signifying our interests and externalizing our points of view. But how can you easily identify which pieces will help to tell your narrative and which ones won't?

For every job I work on, I receive a mood board, a tool often used in creative industries to convey a visual tone. Each client I work with has a unique perspective, which makes it important for me to have a solid understanding of what message they want to communicate before I head out to shop. These boards are crucial to have on hand so I can continually remind myself why I should purchase one piece over another, without allowing my personal tastes to creep in.

Commercial stylists build new wardrobes for every shoot they work on, similar to the way individuals curate their closets. Which is why I want you to use the same concept to home in on what garments and styles excite you.

Don't allow this process to be all-consuming. Instead, listen to yourself and make organic decisions. Are there certain garments your eyes are drawn to? What excites you about a specific look? Try to identify your emotions, and don't be afraid to think critically about the things that revolt you, too.

If there's a piece you would typically wear but don't really love, leave it off the board—this visual isn't about the kind of person you were. It's about communicating to yourself who you are today.

Great outfits are everywhere—walking down the street, on Instagram or Pinterest, or even on your friend's mom. Capture the looks you love and make sure your board is physical so you can look back at it anytime you experience a crisis of faith.

Don't be afraid to ask yourself the tough questions about why a particular look resonates louder than another. Think about colors, materials, silhouettes, and how every garment flatters the body that's wearing it. Does it highlight something you're excited about? Or make you feel like you can't wait to go out to dinner so you can show it off? If it doesn't, kick that image off your board and out of your brain so you can move forward searching for another that does. Love and hate are inextricably connected, which is why figuring out what you don't like can be just as revealing as finding what you do.

Pro Tip: All Sections Are Fair Game

When working on your mood board, don't be afraid to subvert retailers' expectations. Stores typically separate their merchandise by gender because it's what's easiest for them, but it's not all that beneficial for the shoppers who are looking only to buy garments that meet their needs.

One of my female friends spent years feeling out of home in her body because she felt obligated to only purchase pieces designed for women. Wearing these garments gave her the feeling of playing dress-up, as though she was faking her femininity. However, once she allowed herself to try a button-up from the men's section, she immediately felt more secure because it told her narrative instead of one that was foisted upon her.

Consider both men's and women's wear while you're putting together your mood board, and see every garment as fair game. We are living in the twenty-first century, after all—so why do we still

pretend a store's organization means anything more than what it is? Or that we can't walk downstairs because it's "only for men" or upstairs because it's "only for women"?

If a garment makes you feel good, who cares? The confidence you experience while wearing it is way more important than the section you bought it from.

Want to keep everything in one place? Use the next two pages to create your own mood board. Cut photographs out of magazines, draw outfits from memory, print images off your computer, find fabric samples, and tape them all here.

Don't feel like you have to complete your entire board in one sitting. Take the time you need to think, gather, cut, and create. The more time you spend developing your point of view, the quicker it will appear before your very eyes.

SHOP SMARTER, NOT HARDER

Shopping is a waste of time if you feel like you're wasting your time doing it. Before you make any purchases, I urge you to take a minute to reference your mood board so you're sure that what you're buying meets the objectives you've laid out for yourself.

Someone once told me, "There is nothing more oppressive than opportunity!" and they were right. Whether it's finding a new piece at a local boutique or hitting a vintage store, selectivity can be incredibly daunting when such a large part of making a decision means saying no to more than you're saying yes to.

I spent many years, from my early teens to late twenties,

purchasing whatever garments I thought had the wildest patterns, the craziest silhouettes, and the most eye-catching fabrics, because of what I would refer to as their "unique quality." Unfortunately, once I brought these garments home, I always experienced deep regret at not being more discerning with my money. Sure, the sequined gold top with the fringe sleeves was fun, but was it me? It was a critical question I'd forgotten to ask in the dressing room, because I was too excited about the shirt to consider it. However, back in my bedroom, it gained an uncanny ability to shift into something I hadn't anticipated—a garment I could never see myself wearing.

When you waste your time and/or money on something that doesn't support your narrative, the process of shopping can start to feel like a fruitless activity. Negative experiences sit in the body longer than positive ones, and I never want you to have any reservations about getting back out there.

Instead, consider a situation where you encountered a garment you immediately loved, that fit like a glove—both in the dressing room and back home. What worked for you? From your headspace to the layout of the store and the interactions you had with salespeople, consider how you can re-create the very same experience every time you shop.

The more purposeful you are about the pieces you purchase, the more excited you'll be to find more.

Pro Tip: Brand Names Are Bullshit

The framework we once relied upon to understand brand names has eroded under our very eyes. Fashion Week, for example, has seamlessly transitioned from an industry event into an influencer playground. Private shows that were once for buyers and stylists have been redesigned as Instagrammable experiences that rely on viral marketing to perpetuate the notion that brand names are exclusive status symbols.

At the private school where my father taught, I remember being surprised at how many of my classmates believed style lay more in the label than the eye of the beholder. I would watch the girls complain about not having the latest Chanel purse rather than considering if it worked with their outfit or informed their point of view.

The true value of a piece of clothing lies in the way it feels on your frame, but brand names would prefer you felt otherwise. Sure, that new top you bought from Prada is *Prada*, but does it look good on you?

When we allow our individuality and personal preferences to be overlooked in favor of buzz-worthy brand names, we become complicit in perpetuating the hollow sense of status that comes with these types of purchases that oftentimes don't fulfill our needs.

pro tip! IGNORE SALES

Hearing that your favorite store is having a *sale* is almost as exciting as finding out you're up for the lead in the school play or getting a larger tax return than you thought. Unfortunately, unlike both of these examples, sales can often be a bit more insidious than retailers present them to be.

Sales are designed by merchandisers to get you into their store. However, these discounted pieces are often hidden in the basement or the back so you have to walk past all the full-priced garments to get to them in hopes you'll be so taken with at least one (or more!) of their newer pieces that you'll forget the real reason you walked in.

Online sales can be even more cunning, as they frequently feature items that the retailer has had a difficult time selling, whether it be in their store or on the internet. Though purchasing at lower prices can often be tempting, these items are almost always final sale—which means they're probably lemons.

"WHERE'S THE SALE SECTION?"

Even if they're not—the available sizes are often incredibly limited. Because the retailer can refuse to accept returns, it becomes your responsibility to eyeball the garment in hopes you'll choose the right size that best flatters your frame—which even after years of practice and industry experience, I can't do.

Instead, be thoughtful with your purchases and don't be afraid to delete the end-of-season-blowout emails that clutter your in-box. Instead, save your money for when you find garments you love that can be tried in multiple sizes, cuts, and colors. You may end up shelling out more cash up front, but in the long run you're spending far less by not wasting money on items that will sit in your closet and never be worn.

DON'T WAIT TO BUY A GREAT PAIR OF JEANS

I've had the same conversation more times than I can count. Someone will look at me (on set, at a dinner party, or where have you) and ask, "Where can I find a great pair of jeans?"

I'll take their question seriously, list off some of my favorite spots and why I love them, then give an idea of how rises and inseams work and why they're so important to consider when choosing the right fit. Then the person will inevitably turn to me and say, "Thank you so much. I'll keep your advice in mind for when I lose twenty pounds."

Nothing drives me crazier than hearing that. In suggesting they have to wait until they "lose the weight," what they're really saying is that they don't respect themselves enough to invest in something flattering until they become a different person, because who they are now is not worth purchasing anything great for.

When you say negative things about yourself to others, you're communicating something to your body you may not even realize: that for whatever reason, you don't value yourself enough to want to look your best, and your insecurities take precedence over your preferences.

So be kind to yourself and heed my advice. Go out and buy a great pair of jeans. Don't think about what they cost and instead focus on finding ones that make you feel confident and cool. And if you do "lose the weight," I'm happy you met your goal! But you're only going to want to buy a new pair to celebrate.

pro tip! PRIORITIZE YOUR PURCHASES

Retail therapy is fun, but is it fun to realize you just spent more than you intended to satisfy the little voice in your head that said you *needed* to buy that shirt, when really you just *wanted* it? When we shop without a clear idea of what we're looking for, we can easily be swayed to purchase things we later wish we didn't.

Instead, whether it's a day you've set aside for pampering, or a quick look online, always keep a list on hand of exactly what items you'd like to add to your wardrobe. Rank them however you'd like, and be sure to refer to the list often, so you can keep a finger on what you really want to own.

Require a pair of black slacks for an upcoming meeting? Put them at the top of your list. Only wish you had a new jean jacket? Make sure it's closer to the bottom. And if you find the jacket before the slacks, that's great! You can cross the jacket off and add something new.

When you make time to create a list of concrete objectives, you're taking a positive step toward communicating to yourself what your priorities truly are.

CHECKLIST

- ☐ SOME SORT OF BLOUSE
- ☐ COOL PANTS
- ☐ CONTINUE LOOKING FOR THE SHOES OF MY DREAMS EVEN THOUGH I DON'T KNOW WHAT THEY ARE

REVEL IN THE REMIX

From buying designer garments in a boutique to getting your hands on some fast fashion at the mall, shopping online, or picking through a thrift store, there have never been so many options available to help you find the right garments to tell your story. But how do you identify which avenue is right for you? It's all about the remix.

When you eschew the lens through which you've shopped before, you become far more likely to come across clothing that delights and excites you. Any good DJ mixes and arranges the tracks they play, the same way all the best outfits are blended together to incorporate pieces from different retailers. By pairing a vintage belt with a designer skirt and a top from your favorite fast-fashion brand, you're not only saving money, you're also more likely to get your point across because you're choosing pieces that accentuate your style, as opposed to limiting yourself to whatever is available from just one store.

Fast fashion, for example, offers an egalitarian approach the likes of which consumers have never before seen. Pulling from runways and trend reports, these retailers give shoppers opportunities to purchase "designer-like" items at less than half the price of their counterparts, and basics for even lower. Unfortunately, to keep things moving, some corners need to be cut, such as time spent fitting garments on different body types. Often using measurements taken from only one frame, retailers like Zara and H&M tend to size up from there, without pausing to consider how else the garment may need to be augmented.

It can be helpful to identify which fast-fashion retailers take your frame into account. If you know X is always going to offer skirts that work for your height and build, that's an important data point. Or if Y carries jeans that always hit your waist just right, that's another piece of information to keep in your back pocket.

Finding the right designer pieces can be tricky as well, considering the garments sold in stores can easily exceed the money we've earmarked for our clothes. However, online resale can be a key way to subvert this, as numerous retailers now offer platforms that sell high-end pieces for fractions of their initial costs. Though 25 percent off a three-thousand-dollar pair of shoes is still expensive, consumers can often set alerts for the types of prices they're comfortable spending for the pieces they'd like to add to their closets.

Ultimately, mixing different channels will give you a diverse and complex wardrobe to create your outfits from. But it's still up to you to be thoughtful about selecting the right pieces to communicate what you want.

pro tip! THE FIVE COMMANDMENTS OF ONLINE SHOPPING

On an e-commerce set, my role is to make the clothing I work with look like clothing you want to buy. This frequently requires me to fit every garment I style exactly to our model's body. I often use binder clips and other supplies like safety pins to create chains to hold up tube tops, or double-sided tape to fake zippers.

My job is to make sure you'd never know, which is why I always suggest people abide by the following five rules. They may sound simplistic, but I can assure you they'll change the way you use the internet to shop.

1. **Always Buy in Threes:** When purchasing pieces you can't vet in person, always buy three versions of the same garment to try on at home—the size you think will look good, one size up and another below. When your pieces arrive, focus on how they feel on your frame and ignore the size. Choose your favorite, then pack up the other two up and send them right back.

2. **Find Out About Fit:** You can usually tell if an online shop is committed to communicating accurate sizes if they have the specific garment measurements listed. If there's only one size chart that's blanket for the entire website, it's normal for you to feel a little suspicious. Again, be sure to purchase in multiple sizes, and always inspect every picture available (especially the back and sides of the piece). And if there's a video available, watch it! That way, you'll be able to see how the garment moves on the model and can look for anything that could sit awkwardly on you, too.

3. **Use Social Media to Your Advantage:** Many online stores now feature direct links to Instagram posts of their customers wearing different pieces. This can be very helpful if you want to see how garments you're interested in fit on different shapes

and heights, and can give you an idea of how the piece will look on your figure, too.

4. **Shop with a Credit Card:** Not everyone has access, but if you're able to get your hands on a credit card, use it! It will help mitigate the financial strain of buying multiple pieces when you'll ultimately be returning at least two of them.

5. **Examine Your Purchases:** Not all garments are created equal, and it's extremely easy to manipulate an image using light and color. One of the most important things to do before (and after!) buying anything online is to examine the fabric of your new find. It can be tough to know how something will feel just from reading the fiber composition percentages listed online, even if you've taken the time to find them. Once the piece arrives and you're holding it in your hands, the fabric may feel different than you'd imagined. Don't be afraid to ask yourself if the amount you're paying feels equivalent to its quality, and if it's not—send all three pieces back to where they came from.

pro tip! VARY WITH VINTAGE

I love mixing vintage and thrift store pieces into my wardrobe to give it a distinctive feel, and sites like eBay, Etsy, and Poshmark offer consumers a never-ending supply of options. However, buying vintage from an online vendor rarely if ever offers the same flexibility when making a return as buying from a standard retailer does, so you need to be extra careful when you decide to make a purchase.

I suggest taking time to view however many images are available on the listing and inspecting them as closely as possible, making sure to send any questions you have to the seller. Ideally you're looking for garments that are dead stock, that is, pieces that didn't sell at the time of manufacturing and have spent years sitting on warehouse shelves. These items are frequently in much better condition than ones that have been living in someone's closet.

It's also important to inspect your clothing choices when thrifting in the real world, too. While I've been lucky to come across some very special pieces at vintage and thrift stores for fractions of their original sticker price, rarely am I ever able to find out their history. This makes it important for me to check if all the seams are in the right place, how the fabric feels on my skin, and to ask myself if the garment really helps inform the story I'm trying to tell before purchasing it.

Your brain is apt to talk you into buying something just because it's "only two dollars," but if you're not going to wear it, those two dollars could easily be twenty or two hundred dollars.

Only when you've made a conscious effort to accept your body can you begin to dress it.

reinvigorate

If there's one thing I hope you take away from this book, it's that only when you've made a conscious effort to accept your body can you begin to dress it.

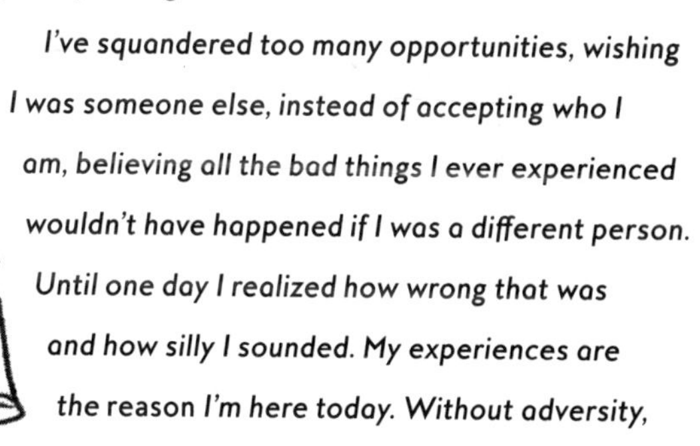

I've squandered too many opportunities, wishing I was someone else, instead of accepting who I am, believing all the bad things I ever experienced wouldn't have happened if I was a different person. Until one day I realized how wrong that was and how silly I sounded. My experiences are the reason I'm here today. Without adversity,

I would not be a successful stylist, who's written a book. I wouldn't be talking to you.

My hope is that in accepting your own past, you will be better equipped to identify how you would like to move forward with your future. The way you dress is an external example of how you think of yourself, and my goal is for every decision you make to affirm the person you are.

I want this book to reinvigorate you to take all the information you've learned and put it to good use. Only you can control the informative nature of your aesthetic, and I'd like to see you stand tall in every outfit you wear.

RETURN WITHOUT REGRET

Did you know the average retailer only ever sees between 10 to 30 percent of their merchandise returned? Yet every person has the opportunity to reconsider their purchases after bringing them home. That means 70 to 90 percent of people are holding on to the clothing they buy, whether they're happy with their investments or still questioning if they made the right choice.

Unlike driving a car off the lot, or saying something we regret, the garments we buy can almost always be taken back. Remember—our purchases have an uncanny ability to shift once unpacked in our bedrooms—but you don't have to live with that sinking feeling in your gut.

Think about the garments you buy as rentals, as opposed to commitments you've made that you can't get out of. It may come as a surprise, but the majority of retailers could care less if you decide to return something to their store.

An even higher percentage of people never return the clothing they buy online because it feels like "too much of a hassle." Per National Public Radio, 91 percent of American online shoppers "only rarely" or "never" return things, while 94 percent say they "only rarely" or "never" make an order expecting to return part of it.

I always tell my clients and friends to build the return process into the way they shop. Instead of going home and immediately ripping off the hang tags, try tucking them into a pocket or hiding them behind your neck until you're unequivocally sure the garment helps inform your narrative.

And if it doesn't—take it back! You might feel like you're on display standing in the return line, but no one's going to get upset, or even remember you were there. Just be sure to take note of the store's return policy so you know how long you have to make your final decision.

Pro Tip: Buy Once, Don't Buy Again

When it comes to finding new garments to add to your wardrobe, only purchase pieces you can see yourself keeping in good condition and wearing for years to come. You don't have to buy a new fall jacket every season or five different types of shoes. And does anyone need seventeen pairs of jeans that just sort of fit? As long as you have two or three that look really good, you're pretty much set.

Our disposable culture prioritizes the notion that the more you're able to buy, the better off you are, but that attitude does not include the cost of maintaining a closet full of clothing you rarely ever put on. From the money needed to launder these pieces to the space they take in your home, there are reasons people say they feel lighter after they get rid of things.

I once had a teacher tell me to never buy a piece of art unless I felt like I couldn't live without it. I urge you to shop by the same rule. Instead of drowning in poorly constructed button-ups and jumpsuits you wish didn't crawl up your butt, try spending more time window-shopping, and purchase new items only when you're sure they'll say exactly what you want them to.

DELINEATE YOUR DESIRES

This is a little trick I like to use when shopping for a shoot. While I always start my process by looking at my client's mood board and making note of their requests, I inevitably come across something I love that doesn't match their vision. Instead of trying to make it work on set and getting disappointed when it doesn't, I think to myself instead, "Oh, this is great . . . for me."

I won't buy the garment, but I will make a mental note or take a picture. And if I can't get it out of my head over the next couple of days, I'll go back to the store and purchase it for myself. By differentiating my client's needs from my own, I find that not only am I more focused while I work but I also buy only what my client wants to see on set.

I encourage you to use the same focus to create a similar barrier between what you respond to and what may be a better fit for somebody else. Do you love the dress in front of you because you know it will look good on your frame? Or would it flatter a friend of yours even more? Take the minute you need to consider, and if it's a better fit for them than you, try texting over an image of the garment instead. It'll still give your brain the satisfaction of picking something out, while also offering an opportunity for you to connect with someone in your life and show a friend they're on your mind.

When you create boundaries, you're much more apt to focus on your own preferences, instead of getting lost in someone else's.

INVENTORY YOUR EXPERIENCES

What makes sense for one person doesn't always work for another, which can be easy to forget when our desires surpass our needs. Instead of giving in to frustration, I suggest you take a step back and inventory your experiences so you can avoid falling into the same traps over and over again.

After every shopping trip, clothing swap, or online browse, take a minute to write down everything that worked for you, while being honest about what didn't. A certain silhouette not accentuate your frame in a way you like? Write it down and get it out of your system.

Take all the bad feelings you have and banish them from your body. Make note of every annoying dressing room experience and each crappy top you wish fit differently. Write a soliloquy to all the dresses you tried that were almost perfect and

the pants that were cut just a little weird. Not only will it help you home in on what makes sense for your body, but you'll also walk away with additional insight into what excites you and an increased sense of confidence when it comes to rejecting the things that don't.

I want you to feel energized every time you think about putting on new clothes and not fear what insecurities they may trigger. By taking time to assess your experiences, you're bound to feel more in control of your wardrobe as opposed to manipulated by it. Because once you have a better understanding of how you would like to organize your shopping experiences, you're much more likely to have positive ones.

pro tip! FIND YOUR VENN

I'm a visual learner who really enjoys charts and graphs, and one of my favorite tools to tap into when I'm struggling with my feelings is the Venn diagram. Use the following one to give yourself insight into the last time you bought something new. What intrigued you, and what do you wish had been different? Were there places those feelings crossed over? Take time to consider the Big Picture, but also what external factors may have impacted your mood. Did you love the layout of X store but couldn't stand their customer service? Would you hit Y again, but only if it was less crowded? Did Z not offer enough options?

Every piece of information you discover is important for charting your intentions and expectations. Accessing what worked and what didn't is necessary in helping you to find the confidence you need to make definitive statements about your style to yourself and others around you.

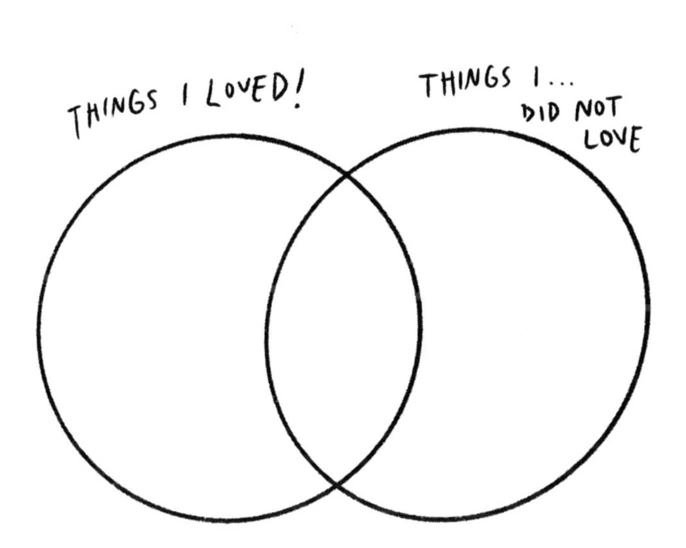
THINGS I LOVED!
THINGS I...
DID NOT
LOVE

NOW GET BACK OUT THERE!

My fashion journey isn't over. It's still developing and changing every day. I am constantly formulating new ideas and recalibrating the way I want to present myself to the world.

Like any good relationship, getting into it isn't the end—it's only the beginning. Over time things will transform, adjust, and grow based on what you need. And when they aren't working? You try something new.

Changing your behavior can be hard, but it's not impossible. It does require a lot of personal work, commitment, and conscious thought, but what good thing doesn't? If you want to alter the way you see something—especially if you've held on to different opinions your entire life—it's going to take some time.

I've tried fad diets to shrink my body. I have hated my hips and blamed them for my insecurities. I spent years with my shoulders hunched inward, because I thought my height made me stick out like a sore thumb. But every time I'd catch myself in a mirror, I would notice how funny I looked. How obvious I was trying to fit in.

When I pitched this book, my goal was to write something that would inspire people who don't care about fashion to care about fashion. Through offering tools that can inspire and be quickly applied I wanted to share what I've learned as a stylist and through my own experiences, but by no means do I think I have all the answers and you have none of them.

I hope you see this text as a rallying cry and a springboard for embracing your own point of view. Instead of wasting your time wishing you were a different person, it's important for all of us to let go of who we think we should be—so that we may enjoy the individuals we already are.

Nothing ever happens the way you think it will. And you can't be upset about it. You just have to roll with the punches. You can't learn what a good decision looks like until you make a bad one.

So go out and make some decisions. Buy things you never thought you would and return them when they don't feel right. Take a chance on a pair of jeans and congratulate yourself when you glance in the mirror and feel confident about the body wearing them. If you like a men's jacket more than a woman's, buy it. Or if you normally wear pants from the men's section, try out a pair of women's jeans—they might fit you better than you'd think.

Make choices. Even when you're afraid of the outcome. Even if you'd rather stay safe.

A failure is only a failure if you don't learn from it. And you have to fail to find out what you don't want, so you can figure out what you do.

Every one of us has a story to tell that's individual, personal, and unique. So stop holding yourself back and start telling yours.

ACKNOWLEDGMENTS

Thank you, Mom, and thank you, Dad; and thank you to my talented editor, Elle Keck; and my wonderful agent, Wendi Gu; and Emma Brodie, who always believed I was the right person to write this book. Thank you to my readers Allie Feras, Tom Hunt, Saskia Nislow, and Mary Ryan. Thank you, Hilary Fitzgerald Campbell, who from the very beginning I wanted to illustrate this project, and to Joe Perri for capturing me just as I want to be seen.

Thank you to every cafe I ever wrote in and every friend I pitched this project to, just so I could pick their brain. Thank you, Logan Halley-Winsett, for giving me my first shot when I was just a kid, and the boys at Anyway Reps for allowing me to take that shot and run with it. Thank you, Rachel Rein, for my first opportunity to style on set, and every photographer, director, producer, and art buyer who has ever taken a chance on me. And to all the talented makeup, hair, prop, food, and set stylists I've collaborated with over the years, I thank you, too.

Thank you, bad experiences, for teaching me what good ones look like, and thank you, hips, for helping me to fall in love with my waist. Thank you, mean boys and cruel girls, without whom I would never have anyone to prove wrong.

And to my teenage self, I say buck up, kiddo. Enjoy the ride. Here's that book you always asked for. I wrote it just for you.

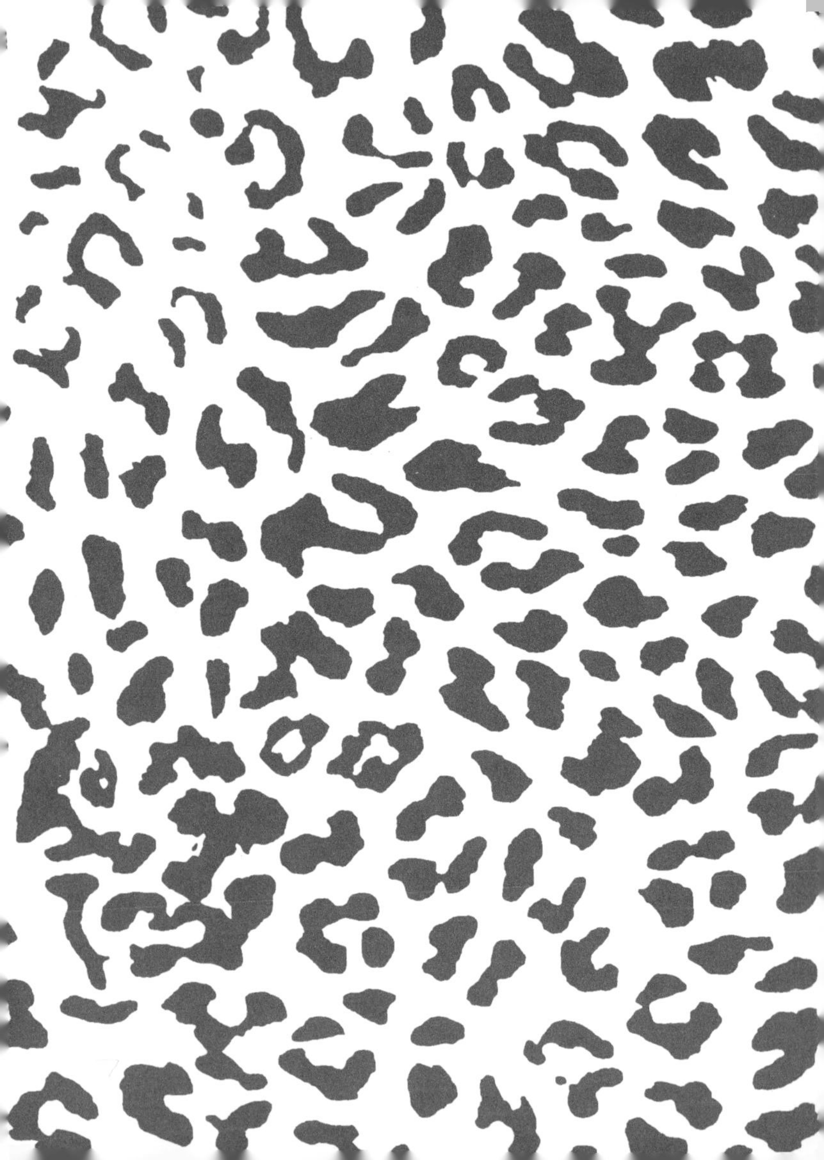